Colour mandalas to increase your concentration. You may also choose to add a focus to your concentration while colouring: perhaps around a topic in your life where you wish to achieve more clarity. For example: "I would like to have greater clarity on what the next steps are towards growing my professional practice. My intention is to know which steps I will take by the time I am finished this mandala."

By focusing your intention you may find that clarity on this topic will increase by the end of the colouring or drawing process.

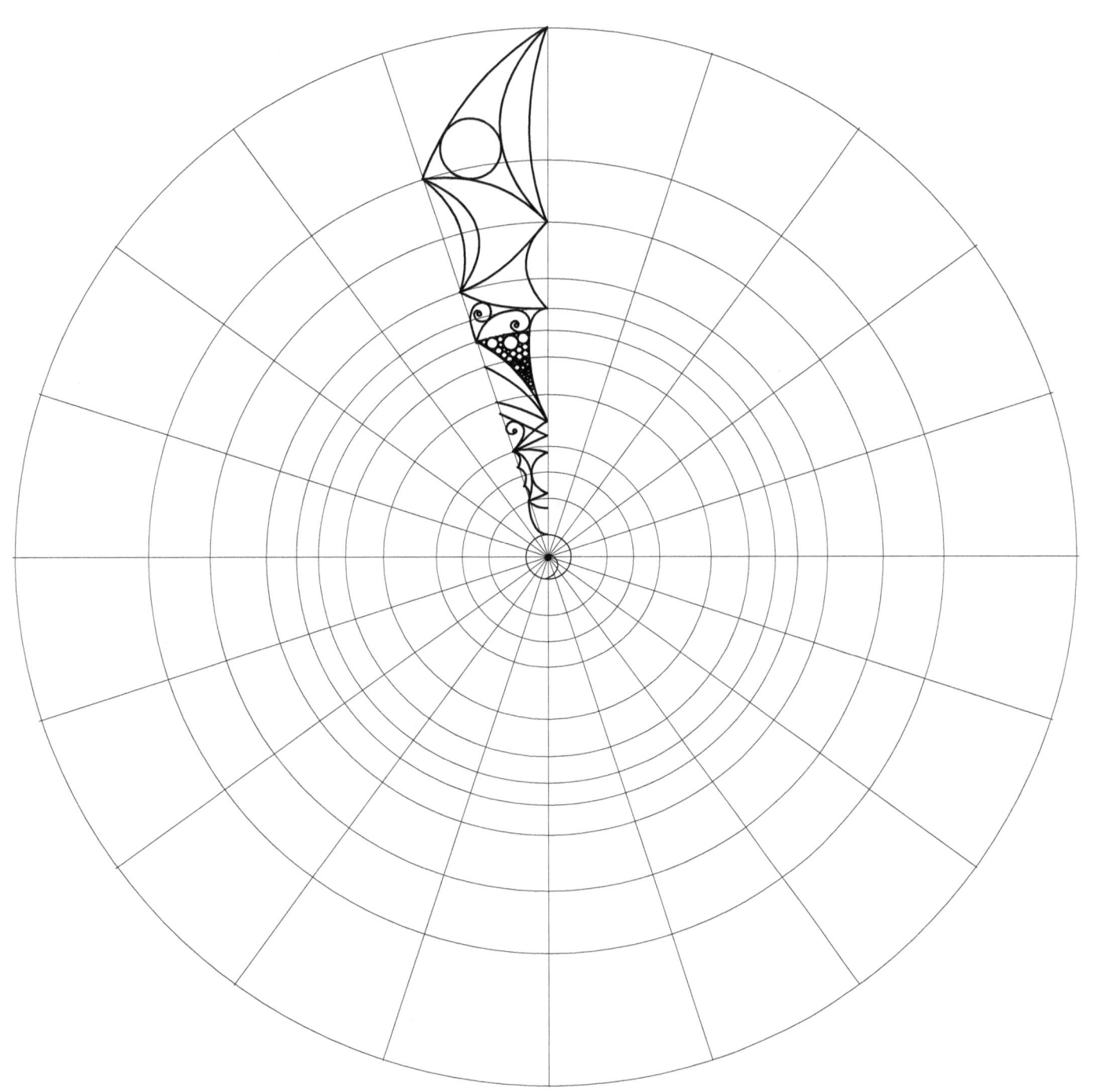

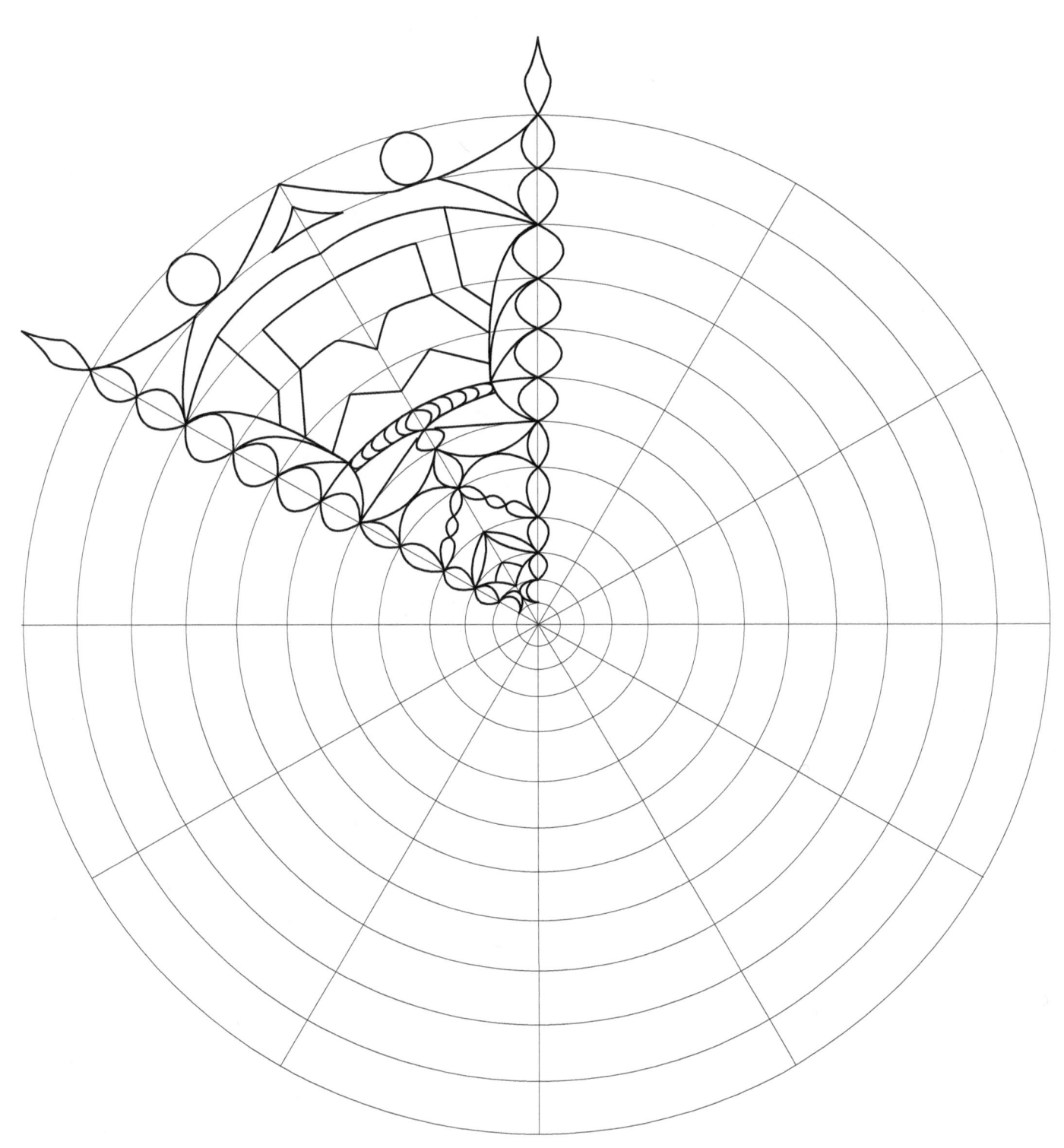

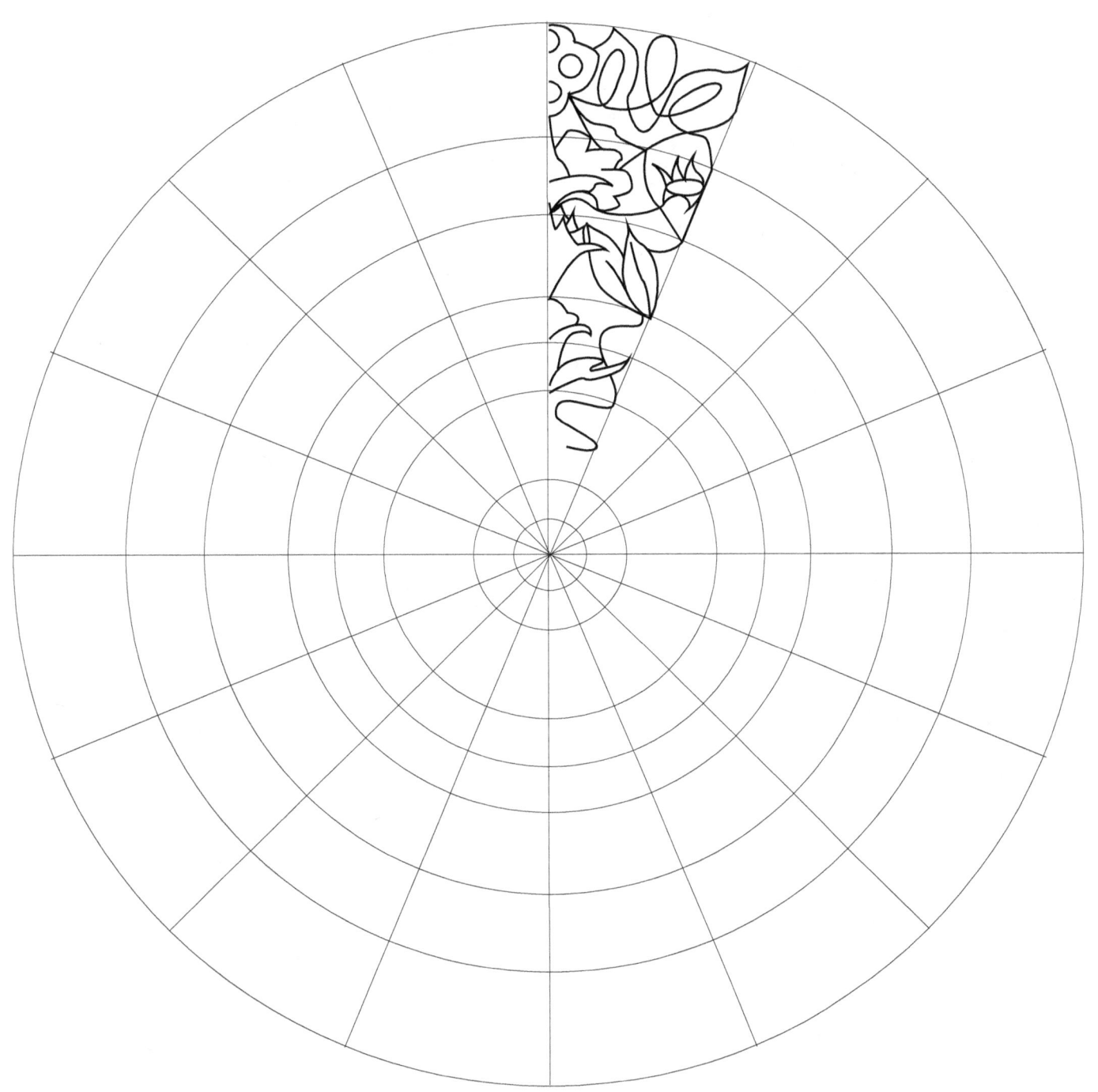

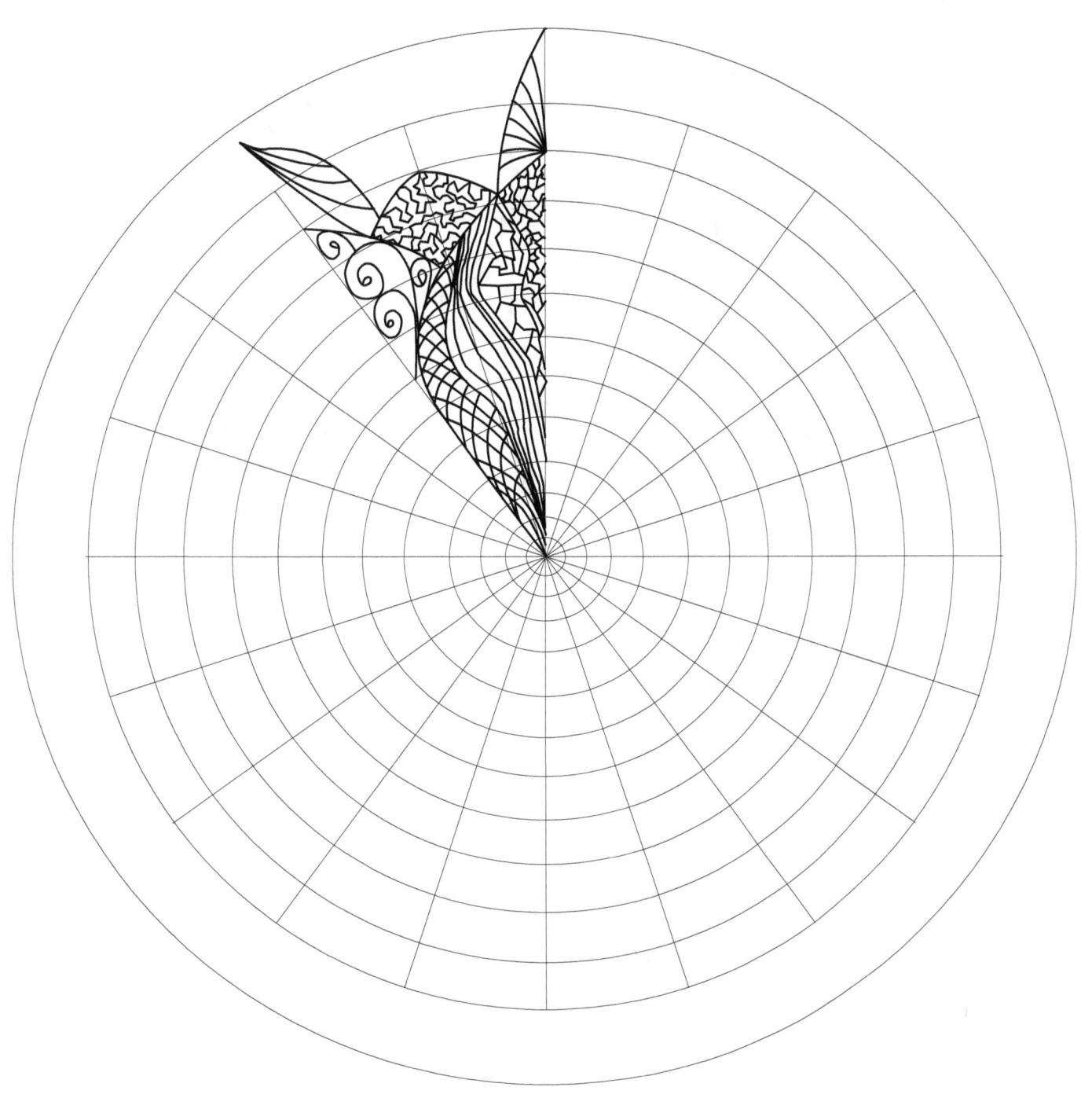

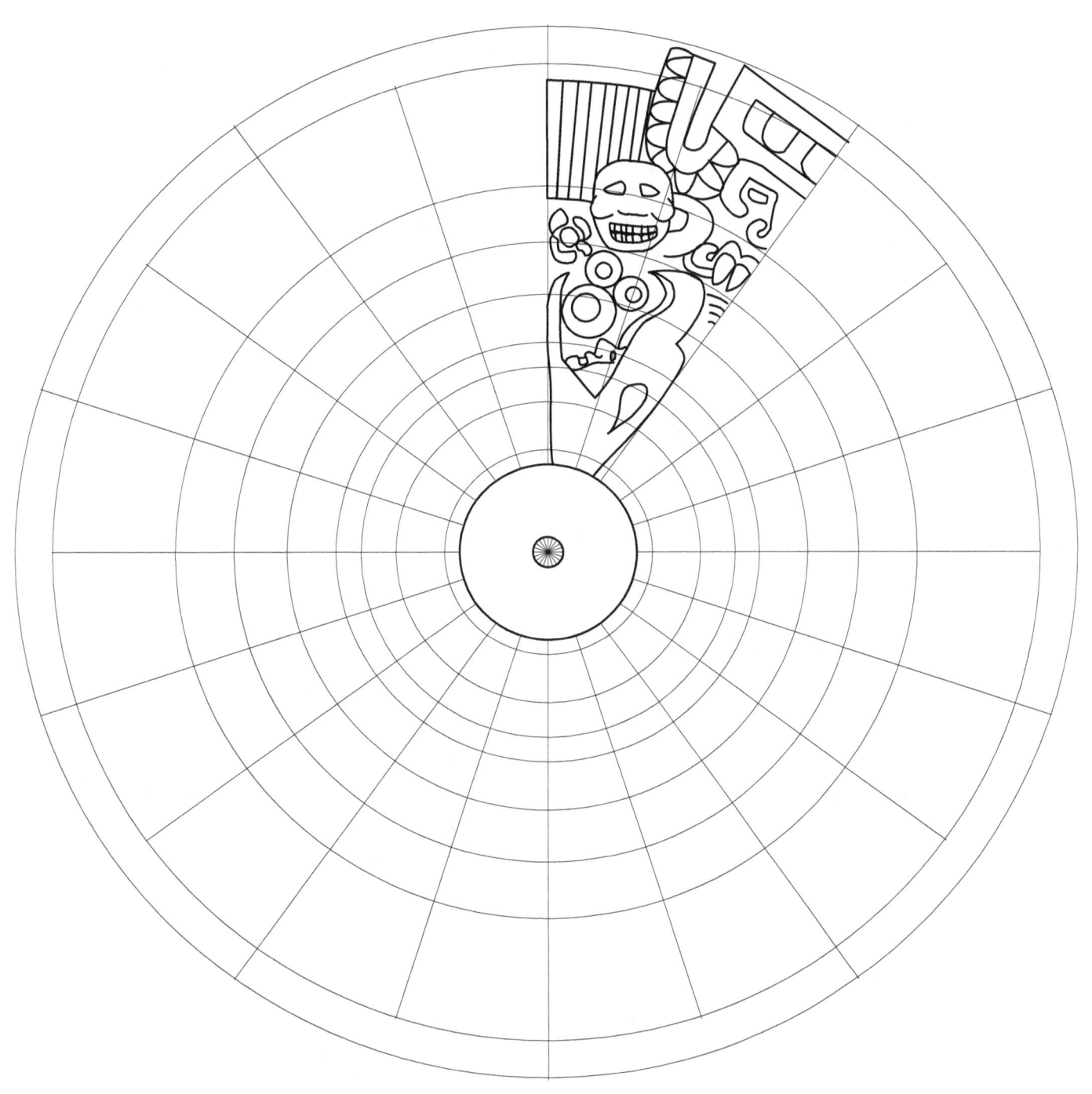

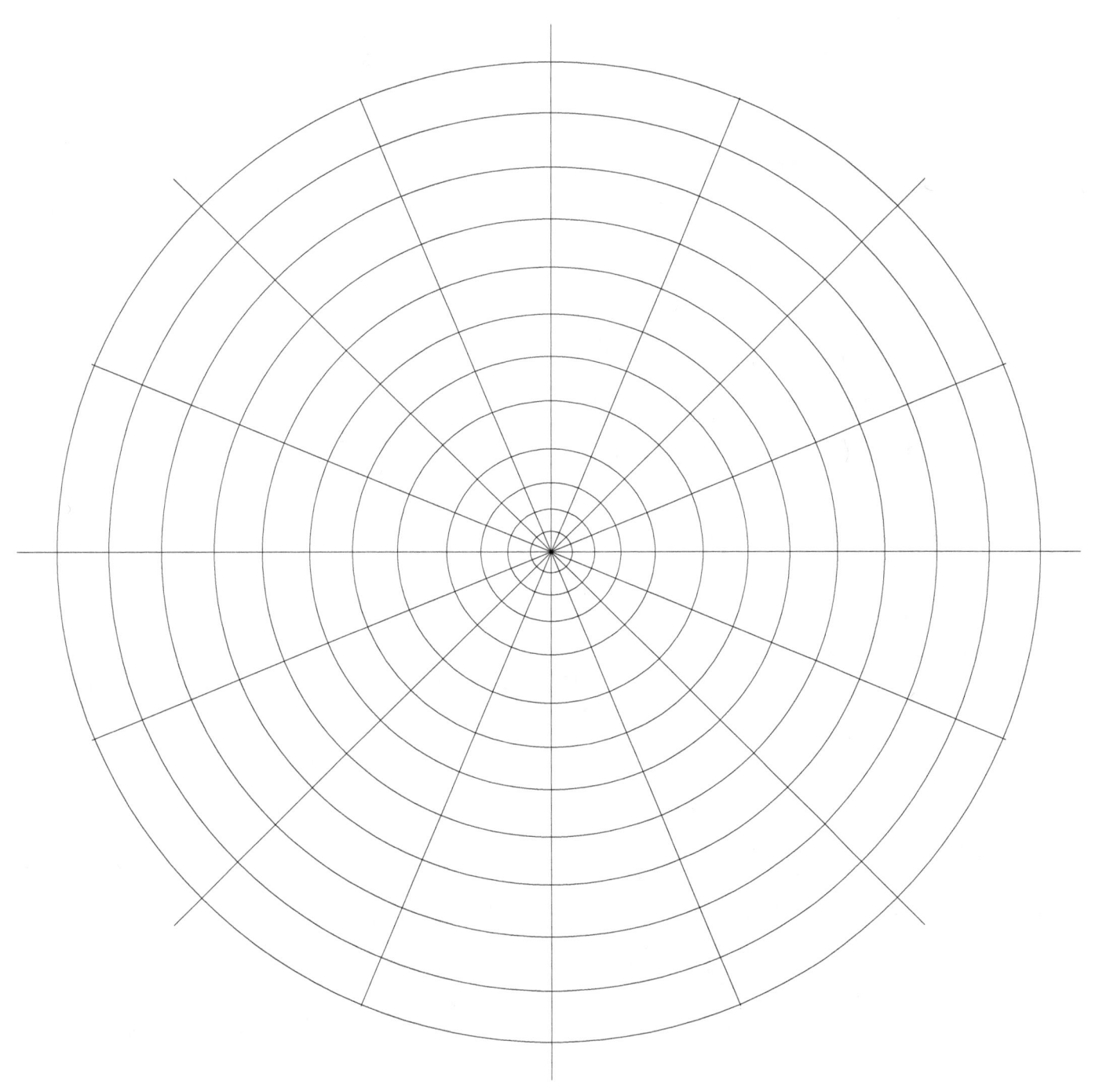

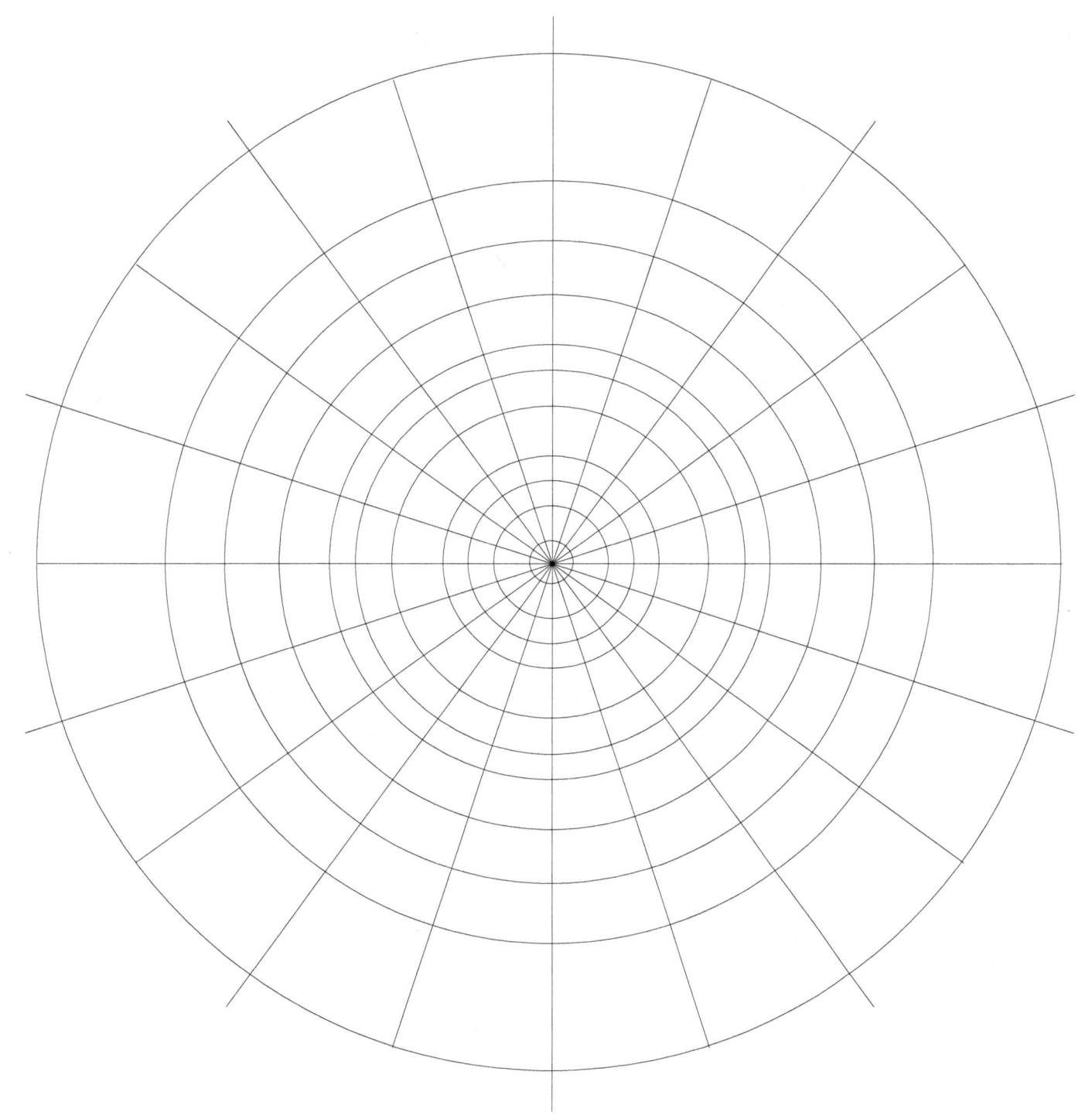

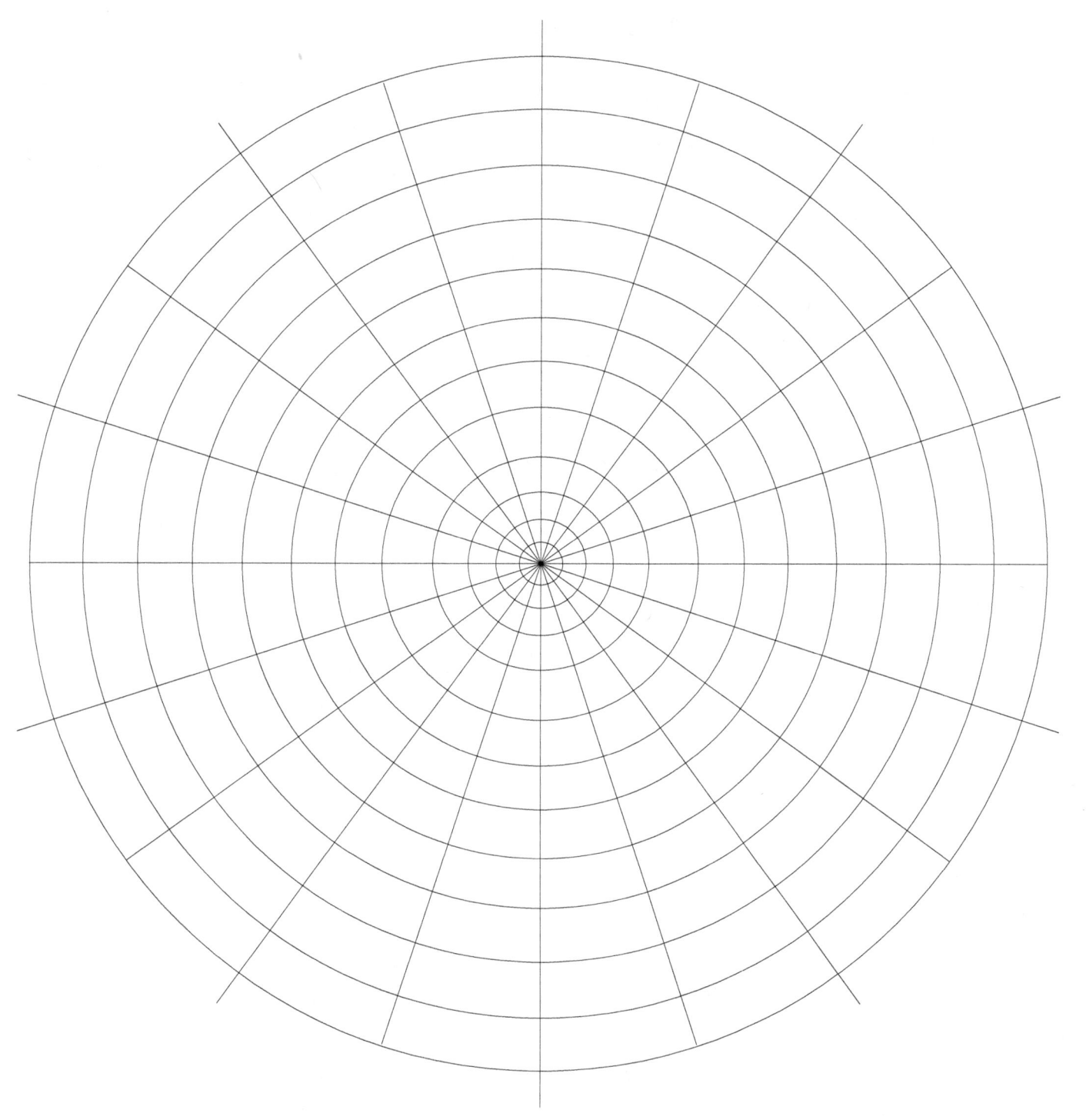

I hope you enjoyed colouring & drawing as much as I enjoyed creating this experience for you. If you feel inspired to share your artwork, you can send a photo or scan of your favourite mandala (coloured or drawn) to my blog. I will publish it in a mandala gallery.

You may choose to have your name published or not, but please include your location.

Send your work to mandalas@rociofatas.org and you will receive a special gift.

© Rocío Fatás, 2015
Depósito Legal: LR 1240-2015
Impreso por Imprenta Vidal
Imprenta Vidal | Avda. Colón, 4 bajo · 26003 Logroño
imprentavidal@fer.es – http://vidalimprenta.com/
Impreso en España – Printed in Spain